NOW THAT YOU ARE AN AN ELDER

by Howard D. Vanderwell

**A study in eldership
for today's church leadership**

Leader's Guide Included

WIPF & STOCK · Eugene, Oregon

Wipf and Stock Publishers
199 W 8th Ave, Suite 3
Eugene, OR 97401

Now That You Are an Elder
A Study in Eldership for Today's Church Leadership
By Vanderwell, Howard D.
Copyright©1990 by Vanderwell, Howard D.
ISBN 13: 978-1-5326-6363-5
Publication date 7/24/2018
Previously published by R.C. Law & Co., Inc., 1990

CONTENTS

INTRODUCTION

SECTION I

SECTION II

LEADERS' GUIDE

Concerning the Office of Elder

T here is a great deal of confusion and ignorance in the church today concerning the office of Elder. That confusion has been fueled by whims of church history which at times has seriously obscured biblical teaching. Such confusion is evidenced today by the fact that some churches have no elders, some have elders with no clear concept of their task, while still others have given them a legitimate and prominent role in the life of the congregation.

Often this deficiency in the church is felt most keenly by the pastor who fails to receive the assistance from elders that he really needs. Most elders do not realize that their office involves the responsibilities of not only supervising the life of the congregation but also assisting the preacher in understanding the needs and concerns of the congregation.

I recently surveyed a number of colleagues in the ministry and discovered that nearly all indicated they would welcome greater assistance from their elders in understanding the needs

1

and concerns of the congregation that must be addressed in preaching. However, as soon as they said that, many were just as quick to express their doubt about the willingness of their elders to provide such assistance.

Therefore, it is critically important for elders to engage in group study about their office. Many enter the office without a clear concept of what is expected of them by Christ, the pastor, or the congregation. They are either overwhelmed by the task and thereby begin to consider it a monstrous burden, or fail to catch a sufficient vision of how God desires to use them in the life of the congregation and thereby greatly reduce their effectiveness as leaders. For such individuals group study provides a healthy opportunity for growth and will give them a forum in which they are able to share insights with each other and will assure the congregation of better trained leadership for years to come.

MY ASSUMPTIONS

I am making several assumptions throughout these studies that ought to be set out at the beginning. I am convinced that the pattern prescribed for the New Testament church calls for a plurality of leaders. The stability and health of the church is served best by such an arrangement. Therefore I am convinced that the form of church government which calls for the church to be ruled by a body of lay leaders (called Elders) is the most biblical concept. Historically this has been called the "presbyterian" form of church government, from the Greek word PRESBUTEROS which means "elder."

My viewpoint is that basically there are two major offices in the church—those of elder and deacon. Where tasks are more carefully delineated the office of elder is divided between that of teaching elder (pastor), ruling elder, and, in some instances, evangelist. However, care must be taken that the essential oneness of this office is always affirmed.

The distinction between the office of elder and the office of deacon is that one is responsible for the supervision of the spiritual life of the congregation and the other is responsible for the ministry of mercy both to the congregation and the community. The *Church Order* of my denomination (The Christian Reformed Church) sets forth the distinction between these two offices in this way:

> The elders, with the minister(s), shall have oversight of the doctrine and life of the members of the congregation and fellow officebearers, the exercise of admonition and discipline, the pastoral care of the congregation, participation in and the promotion of evangelism, and defense of the faith." (Art. 24)

> The deacons shall represent and administer the mercy of Christ to all people, especially to those who belong to the community of believers, and shall stimulate the members of Christ's church to faithful, obedient stewardship of their resources on behalf of the needy – all with words of biblical encouragement and testimony which assure the unity of word and deed. (Art. 25)

Though it is our purpose here to focus on the office of elder, we must remember its distinction from the office of deacon. The clarification of such distinctions has become so necessary because there is significant variety in the terms that various churches use. When you hear churches speak of their elders, or deacons, or trustees, or use other titles, it is not safe to assume that we are using such terms in the same way. Consequently, it is important for me to clearly identify the terms I am using and the definitions I am assuming.

Our concern, of course, focuses on the elders, and it must be noted that it is often very easy for churches to shift greater responsibility for the life of the church to the full-time elders, i.e., the pastors, and to allow part-time elders to assume less and less responsibility. On the one hand, this is natural because the pastor is full-time in a leadership role. On the other hand, we must recognize something very unhealthy and unbiblical in this tendency, for the significance of all elders must never be eclipsed.

Though historically there have been those who hold to a life-time eldership and others who hold to a term eldership, the church tradition with which I am associated and out of which I speak calls for a three year term for elders. Though the biblical material does not conclusively settle this question one way or the other, it seems to me that practical considerations point to the wisdom of term eldership. However, that does not preclude the possibility that in complex matters or in long range planning the church may desire to draw on the insights and experience of those who are presently non-active elders.

HISTORICAL DEVELOPMENT

Our purposes here do not require a detailed analysis of the history of the office of elder, but it is necessary for us to have a general idea of how our understanding of the office has come into being.

The Old Testament includes many references to the "elders of Israel" beginning already with Moses. Such elders were involved with Moses and Aaron in conveying the Word of God to the people, in representing the people before God on certain occasions, and in administering local government as well as national affairs. They achieved greater prominence during the Exile and after the Return and became associated with the Judges in administering and executing justice. In the Maccabean period the title "Elders of Israel" was used of the members of the Jewish Sanhedrin.

Their central role in the life of the church appears much more clearly in the New Testament. Paul called for the appointment of elders in every church and gave guidelines concerning their tasks and qualifications. Peter also gives exhortations concerning the manner in which they are to carry out their tasks. It becomes clear, therefore, that the developing New Testament Church was led by a plurality of elders.

In the centuries that followed, however, this lay administered organization of the church gradually underwent a fundamental change. The Church seemed unable to accept and distinguish this office of elder from that of deacon. At some points the church focused on the work of elders and at other times on the work of deacons, but seemed unable to develop the ministry of both side by side. Sometimes the whole idea of lay leadership was rejected.

During the first four centuries the diaconate gained an increasing role of prominence, and the hierarchical structure which still characterizes the Roman Catholic Church came into being. The diaconate functioned as administrative assistants to the bishop and took on increasing liturgical responsibilities. After the fourth century the diaconate decreased in function and the eldership increased, eventually becoming an order of priests. Over several centuries, therefore, the office of elder as it functioned in the early church was lost, the distinction between ruling and teaching elders was no longer considered valid, and all attention and authority was focused on the hierarchical structure of priests and bishops.

At the beginning of the sixteenth century the time was right for a change and a mighty religious movement that we have come to know as the Protestant Reformation swept across Europe. Its original purpose was not to start a new church but to cleanse the existing one from abuses and impurities. The faith of the New Testament church was reexamined and discovered anew. The full system of Christian Truth was once again set before the people. And a new examination of the organization and structure of the church was also a part of that effort and brought some fundamental changes.

John Calvin, one of the primary leaders of that movement, did much in his writing and preaching to carry the minds and hearts of the people back to the early Christian Church. Since the earliest Church was not carefully or clearly organized, Calvin focused his thoughts about structure on the church of the second century and taught that Christ had instituted four offices in the church: pastors who were to preach the Word of God; teachers who were to establish schools for the education of the young and old; ruling elders to maintain order and discipline; and deacons who were to administer charities for the poor.

Calvin was convinced that the elders of the church at Geneva should correspond closely to the "elders of the people" of the Old Testament. Consequently he clarified the policy for such a ruling body. In Geneva he established a ruling body consisting of twelve laymen representing various parishes in the city. These men took an oath similar to that of ministers and met each week with the pastors in a body known as the consistory to supervise the spiritual life of the congregation.

Churches in the Presbyterian and Reformed family have followed the lead of Calvin, though with some variations. Generally, however, they have been agreed on a number of principles concerning the government of the church: first, that leadership of the church should be vested in a plurality of leaders, second, that the plurality of leaders should be drawn from the local congregation, third, that there should be a distinction between ruling elders (who are responsible for the supervision of the church and its life) and teaching elders (who are responsible for preaching and teaching the Word of

God), and finally, that there should be a distinction between lay leaders called elders who supervise the life of the church and deacons who are responsible for the ministry of mercy.

THEIR TASKS

We have seen now that it is necessary for the church to benefit from the leadership of a plurality of elders. Even though the office of ruling elder and teaching elder was not clearly distinguished in the early church, and even though the tasks of elders are not precisely outlined in the New Testament, it is very well possible for us not only to reach the conclusion that Christ intended for elders to be present in every church, but also the general direction in which their responsibilities lie.

There are fourteen different words used in the New Testament in reference to the activity of elders. Some are more precise than others, but all together give us the clear impression that the functions of elders included four areas of responsibility.

The first area of responsibility is that of *nurturing the spiritual life of the congregation.* In I Peter 5:1,2 the elders are exhorted by Peter, "... a fellow elder ...," to "Be shepherds of God's flock that is under your care...." It is important that we understand Peter's willingness to link the concept of shepherd and elder so closely that they can be regarded as synonymous. A shepherd is preoccupied with feeding and caring for the flock and as such is intended to be a model for elders. A little later, in verse three, Peter sees the elders feeding and nurturing the sheep by setting their own wholesome example before them. In other words, their own lives are to function as a blueprint by which the members of the church may know how to structure their own lives. In Titus 1:9 Paul commands that elders must be willing and able to "... encourage others by sound doctrine...," that is, by feeding and nourishing them well on the truths of the Christian faith so they will be led to greater obedience and action. In I Thessalonians 5:12, Paul asks them to respect those who "... work hard among you ..." and the word that Paul has selected (KOPIOUNTAS) is one that emphasizes the hard labor of concentrated effort to build someone up so that they might be productive and creative. Elders, therefore, must see the church as those who need to be nurtured well in the truth so that they will be obedient in their Christian service.

Secondly, they must *defend the church*. The body of Christ needs nurture in order to become productive; but must also be protected from enemies that aim to sabotage its health and existence. Therefore, the New Testament writers employ a number of terms that reflect the defensive stance that elders must take as they aim to protect the body of Christ. When Paul met with the elders from Ephesus at Miletus, he exhorted them to be faithful in their task. "Guard yourselves and all the flock of which the Holy Spirit has made you overseers" (Acts 20:28). The word he selected means to constantly hold the mind ready to detect and defend against possible threats. Because false prophets, Pharisees, and other evil workers distort truth and destroy the church, the elders must stand guard. In exhorting them to be on their guard Paul selects a word that involves keeping wide awake and zealously alert to all possible threats. He warns them that the church will not have an easy road to travel in the world. Savage wolves will enter among the flock and even from within their number some will arise to sabotage the life of the church. The author of Hebrews employs the same term to describe leaders as those who "... keep watch over you as men who must give account" (Hebrews 13:17) Under those circumstances, elders who take a defensive stance are urgently needed.

A third area of responsibility is the *provision of corrective care*. Not all the difficulties of the church are potential, or outside the church. Some have already inflicted their damage and have led members of the church in the wrong direction. Correction, therefore, is another important ingredient of the task of faithful elders. To the Thessalonians, Paul describes the elders not only as those who work hard among them, being over them in the Lord, but also as those who "... admonish them" (I Thessalonians 5:12). The word he selects indicates a ministry of strong verbal warning and instruction about the dangers, weaknesses and failures that are present; a warning that arises out of a warm and loving spirit deeply concerned about their welfare. In Titus 1:9 Paul describes elders as those who must not only be able to encourage others by sound doctrine but also to "... refute those who oppose it." He is pointing to the activity of making an issue so clear that the person being confronted will come under conviction. When Paul describes the function of the God-breathed Scriptures in II Timothy 3:16, he selects this term again. So elders frequently find themselves involved in the firm and loving correction that is needed in the body of Christ.

The final responsibility of church elders is to *provide directional leadership*. Another family of terms employed in the New Testament leads us to picture elders as those who exercise their leadership by setting the direction for the church and its members. In the passage that we previously noted as the watershed for distinguishing the two types of elders (I Timothy 5:17) Paul calls them those "... who direct the affairs of the church...." He uses a participle with an adverb to give us a picture of someone who serves as an excellent director, standing at the head of a congregation, and leading it in the right direction. When he speaks to the Thessalonians about "... those who are over you in the Lord...." (I Thessalonians 5:12) he sketches a word picture of a superintendent who manages them in such a way that they become productive. In his listing of spiritual gifts Paul includes the gifts of "administration" (I Corinthians 12:28) and "leadership" (Romans 12:8). Both of these terms infer responsibilities concerning the course of direction in which a group moves, whether it be a ship at sea directed by its captain, or an organization that is directed by its leader. Elders, therefore, are responsible for the direction that the church takes.

It is not possible for us to know exactly how and in what way the elders carried out these four dimensions of their task because the terms in Scripture are very general. Nevertheless, it is very clear that their role was an important one in each of these four dimensions, and the church cannot expect to be as healthy and productive as Christ intends it to be unless faithful elders are present.

These Study Guides are made available with the prayer that the church and her lay leaders may gain a better understanding of this office and be more adequately equipped to fill it.

SUGGESTED METHOD FOR THIS STUDY

The material that is presented here is designed for use by the elders in study sessions. There are several forms that this study session may take.

(1) Some groups may prefer to use the study as a *devotional session* at each monthly Elders meeting. If this plan is followed I strongly suggest that this group study be the first item of the evening. Then its insights will set the tone for the entire evening and there will be less risk of a full evening's agenda squeezing it out.

Because there is an abundance of material in each lesson, you have to consider the option that you prefer. Some spend two study sessions on each lesson, taking half each time. Others are selective and study only certain questions of each lesson. Others have sufficient time to cover an entire lesson in one study session.

(2) Some groups may prefer to use this material in a *workshop/retreat setting*. A day, or more, away from regular agendas often provides a much better opportunity for in-depth discussions and study. In such a setting a number of appropriate lessons can be covered at one time. The effect will be cumulative.

The material is arranged in two sections containing six lessons each. It is intended that the material be used as a whole, however it is possible to separate the two sections and use only one of them. The greatest benefit, of course, will come when they are used together. Section I lays the foundation for our understanding of the office of elder, and Section II leads us in personal preparation and nurture in the task and is intended as a sequel to the first Section.

Each lesson requires three ingredients and the greatest benefit will be experienced only when all three ingredients are present.

(1) **Prior preparation by each participant.** The homework required should include a study of the designated Scripture passage(s) and personal reflection and response to the thought questions.

(2) **Structured presentation by a leader.** The leader may be either the pastor or a designated elder but he should be one who is capable of reviewing for the group the pertinent biblical material and any church regulations that bear on the subject. (Please note the "Leader's Guide" included at the end, for assistance to the Leader.)

(3) **Group discussion.** Here the participants have an opportunity to share the insights they have gained from their personal study and experience, raise their questions, and engage in evaluations of the current method of functioning as elders.

The body of elders who engage in such a study will find their work as elder much more fulfilling and rewarding. Their pastor will benefit from their valuable assistance. And the congregation will receive the benefits of greater leadership. Such positive benefits will certainly advance the cause of Christ and the health of the Church today.

The Nature of The Office

LESSON 1 – Appointed Elders

Scripture References: Exodus 3:16-22
Acts 14:21-28
Titus 1:5-9

Throughout the Old Testament the "Elders of Israel" appear frequently. Though no precise definition of their responsibilities is given, it is obvious that much of the care of the people of God had been placed in their hands. In the New Testament, as soon as the Apostles established new Christian churches, they called for Elders to be appointed. Theirs was a special task and the "Laying on of Hands" set them aside for that task.

1. Reflect on Exodus 3.

   a. What were the circumstances among the people of Israel and in the life of Moses?

b. What was Moses' task in that setting?

c. How did God specifically equip him for that task?

d. What was the relationship between Moses and the Elders?

e. Why was it necessary that there were elders in Israel? (Consult a Bible Dictionary or Bible Encyclopedia for information about Old Testament Elders.)

2. Reflect on the Acts 14 and Titus 1 passages and note the charge that is given to appoint Elders.

   a. Why do you suppose that was so important to the disciples?

   b. What do you think their tasks were?

   c. How would the church be different today if there were no elders?

3. There are a number of biblical references to the "laying on of hands" for the spiritual leaders of the church. Consult such references as Acts 6:6; 8:18; 13:3; I Timothy 4:14; 5:22; and II Timothy 1:6.

a. What do you think the "laying on of hands" meant to the church? to the newly appointed elders?

b. One church has said, "The ceremony of the Laying on of hands symbolizes the appointment of a person as the representative of the group which has laid hands on him. After such a ceremony the person appointed acts on behalf of the group and on the authority of the group.

The group has empowered him to use in their name certain divinely bestowed gifts which they recognized in him.... In the laying on of hands, therefore, we have a ceremony which the New Testament church sometimes used for publicly confirming its call and appointment of certain people to special ministries." (*Acts of Synod of the Christian Reformed Church 1973*)

Discuss the significance of that practice for your present situation. Have you experienced the laying on of hands? If so, what did it mean for you? If not, are there benefits that would come from it?

LESSON 2 – The Nurture We Provide

Scripture References: I Peter 5:1-4
                                    Acts 20:32-38

"Nurture" and "feed" are big words in the Bible. In the Gospel of John Jesus is presented as the Living Water (John 4:13,14) so that we may never thirst again, the Bread of Life (John 6:35) so that we may never go hungry again, and the Vine (John 15:5) so that we may bring forth much fruit. As soon as Peter was restored after his denials he received the charge to "Feed my sheep" (John 21:15-19). Elders and Shepherds are two terms so closely linked in the New Testament that they ought to be considered synonyms.

1. Reflect on I Peter 5:1-4.

   a. Think of yourself as a Palestinian shepherd on the hills of Judea with your flock of sheep. What would you aim to do for them in order to be considered a faithful and successful shepherd? What would be of the greatest importance to you?

   b. Now transfer that scene to your local congregation and again ask what you should do for the members of your congregation in order to be considered a faithful and successful elder?

   c. On the basis of that reflection, write down three things that you consider to be of greatest importance for the members of your congregation.

      1.)

      2.)

      3.)

d. According to Peter, what mistakes could you make that might sabotage your effectiveness?

e. What do you understand by the "crown of glory" and when will you receive it?

2. Reflect on Paul's farewell comments to the Ephesian Elders in Acts 20.

a. In what ways had Paul been a model or example for them?

b. Why do you suppose Paul speaks to these elders about being "built up?" Are there special needs that elders have? If so, what are some of them?

3. Develop a clear presentation of the Gospel based upon Scripture. Know it so well that you can share it with someone whenever the opportunity arises. If you have done so, share with your fellow elders one recent instance in which you have shared it with someone.

a. What was the hearer's response?

b. How did you feel about it?

4. How well can you use the Bible to counsel others?

a. Can you cite a passage you would use to counsel someone about the assurance of salvation?

b. What passage or promise would you use to counsel someone who is burdened with guilt?

c. What passage or promise would you use to counsel someone who is discouraged and feels defeated?

d. What passage or promise would you use to encourage someone who has given up on praying?

e. What passage or promise would you use to comfort someone who knows he/she is dying?

f. What passage or promise would you use to give direction to someone facing a critical decision?

g. What passage or promise would you use to comfort someone who has just lost a loved one?

LESSON 3 – The Defensive Stance We Take

Scripture References: Acts 20:25-31
                           II Corinthians 11:1-15
                           Hebrews 13:17

The Spirit has often warned the church about the fact that she lives now in hostile territory. Satan did his best to stop Christ from going to the Cross. Now Satan aims his best efforts at destroying the health and effectiveness of the Christian Church. We are warned about savage wolves that will come in (Acts 20:29), a roaring lion looking for someone to devour (I Peter 5:8), those masquerading as angels of light (II Corinthians 11:14), and false prophets with destructive heresies (II Peter 2:1). Elders, therefore, have an urgent responsibility to defend the church from such dangers.

1. Read Paul's warnings to the Ephesian Elders again – Acts 20:25ff.

   a. What threats does the church face today that have been common to all centuries of the church?

   b. What unique threats does the church face today in our community about which we ought to be concerned?

   c. What circumstances in the church today cause you the most tears? (Note Paul's admission in v. 31.)

2. Notice how Paul, in II Corinthians 11, refers to the tactic of Satan in which he masquerades himself as an angel of light. Do you see that happening in the church today?

   If so, how and where?

3. In Hebrews 13:17 leaders are described as people who "keep watch over you as men who must give account." The word that verse uses means a wide-awake stance that will spot even the first appearance of danger and meet it. Cite three ways in which you and the other elders are currently "keeping watch." How adequate do you feel those efforts are?

   a.

   b.

   c.

4. The church has usually held that one of the functions of preaching is that of defending the truth against error. Therefore it is important that elders assist pastors in determining which errors must be exposed and which needs in the congregation must be addressed.

   a. List two issues of Christian doctrine or teaching that you believe must be addressed in preaching during the next few months because your members may be confused or misled about them.

   b. List two matters of morals or ethics that you believe must be addressed in preaching during the next few months because your members may be confused or misled.

   c. In a spirit of loving assistance, give your pastor some suggestions on how you believe each of these can be addressed most effectively.

LESSON 4 – The Corrective Care We Provide

Scripture References: I Thessalonians 5:12-15
                        II Timothy 3:16,17
                        Titus 1:5-9

Because error and sin frequently appear in the life of the Christian and the Christian Church, correction is needed. But the church uses different tools for that correction than other institutions do. Others may use a show of force and the threat of punishment. But the church uses words that come from a warm and loving spirit that is genuinely concerned about the well-being of those who need the correction. The ministry of admonition, therefore, becomes very important and requires skillful efforts.

1. Read II Timothy 3:16,17 and notice how Paul describes the function of the inspired Scriptures.

   a. Describe what you think it means to be "thoroughly equipped" (v. 17).

   b. List the four kinds of "usefulness" the Bible has in order to equip us thoroughly (v.16). Be sure you understand each term.

2. The word Paul selects in I Thessalonians 5:12 ("admonish") refers to the practice of verbally confronting someone concerning error in their thinking or living and exhorting them to bring it into line with what is correct.

   a. Can you think of a time when that was done to you?

b. How did you feel about it at the time? How did you respond? How did you feel about it later?

c. What could you learn from that about how to handle the responsibility to admonish others?

d. Can you cite a recent example of how your duties as an elder called you to admonish someone for wrong in their life?

   1.) How did you feel about doing that?

   2.) How did they respond to it?

   3.) How could you have done it better?

e. How does the fact that Paul describes leaders as those "who are over you in the Lord" influence the manner in which such admonition should be carried out?

3. Consult Titus 1:9 and notice that Paul now uses a stronger word – "refute." A refutation is a verbal effort that makes an issue so clear that even though someone may not agree with you they know they have been confronted with the truth.

a. Can anyone in the group cite an instance in the past year or two in which you were called upon to refute someone's error.

b. Where do you anticipate that you may have to do that in the future?

4. How well can you use the Bible to correct others?

a. What passage of Scripture would you use to confront someone who refuses to worship faithfully?

b. What passage would you use to confront someone who is unfaithful to his/her marriage vows?

c. What passage would you use to confront someone who is presently living in broken relationships toward others?

d. What passages would you use to confront someone who is disobedient to his/her parents?

5. What are the most difficult aspects of confrontation for you and for others you know? What makes them so difficult?

LESSON 5 – The Directional Leadership We Give

Scripture References: Ephesians 4:1-16
                      I Timothy 5:17
                      II Timothy 2:1-7

Leadership might be called "a headmanship." It is not a process of pushing. What happens when you push a rope? Someone has to set the direction in which the church will go. Churches that show no movement show little life. But movement requires leadership. If the direction of the church is left to everyone's wishes, the church will be fragmented and will move in no unified direction at all. If those who are given the responsibility of leadership have no clear sense of direction themselves, the church could well move...but in the wrong direction. In his concern for the church, therefore, Christ has called certain individuals to be direction-setting leaders. To be such a leader one's personal sense of direction must be clear and one's ability to communicate that to others must be evident and trusted. He must be able to stand at the head of a group and function as one who encourages it in the proper direction.

1. Reflect on Paul's statements in Ephesians 4 again.

   a. How do individuals receive different gifts?

   b. What, according to Paul, are the main tasks of church leaders?

   c. After reflecting carefully on vss. 12-16, make a list of the ingredients that you think are essential for a church to qualify as being "built up."

2. What do you believe Paul has in mind in I Timothy 5:17 where he describes Elders as those who "direct the affairs of the church well"?

   a. Cite one instance in your experience where a group of Elders gave exceptionally good "directional leadership" which made a wholesome difference in the life of the congregation.

   b. What "honor" is Paul talking about in this verse? From whom does it come?

3. Now read II Timothy 2:1-7 very carefully and make a list of the qualifications that are needed to be an effective church leader. How many can you find in those verses?

4. As a group, make an attempt to formulate your own definition of leadership. Each person should complete these sentences and share thoughts about the matter with the others.

   "Leadership is....

   "Leadership happens when....

5. Discuss these questions on the basis of the present circumstances in your congregation.

   a. What major concerns must your congregation face in the next three years?

   b. What preparation should be made now so that those concerns can be met successfully?

   c. How would you describe the direction in which the life of your congregation is presently moving?

   d. What influence does the preaching ministry of your congregation have on that direction, and what could you do to assist your pastor in that?

   e. What influence does the educational ministry of your congregation have on that direction, and what could be done to improve that?

LESSON 6 – The Reception We Can Expect

Scripture References: I Thessalonians 5:12,13
                            I Timothy 5:17-20
                            Hebrews 13:17

Leadership is always a two-way street. It takes people who are called and willing to be leaders. But it also takes those who are willing to be led. Often leadership efforts fail because highly qualified leaders were not accepted, and the group refused to follow. Therefore, the Bible not only speaks about the tasks and qualifications of those who lead, but the reception they can expect to receive from the members of the Body of Christ.

1. Read I Thessalonians 5:12,13 very carefully.

    a. In what ways do you feel that you have been held in "respect" and "highest regard" by the members of the congregation in which you serve?

    b. Are there times when you have not received the proper respect? Describe the kind of situation in which that happened.

2. Read I Timothy 5:17-20 and note what Paul says there about the respect that a spiritual leader can expect.

    a. Examine his statement about "double honor" in v. 17. Check this in several translations and consult some commentaries. What do you think this means? What light does v. 18 shed on it?

    b. How and where do you see "double honor" being extended in your congregation?

c. From time to time accusations and criticisms are made against Elders. Examine v. 20 for the procedure that is to be followed in such instances. What is that procedure?

d. Why do you think it is so important that accusations against elders be handled properly?

3. The instruction of these passages assumes that Elders will be persuasive leaders. In that light evaluate the present functioning of your body of Elders. Would you say that you have attempted to be too persuasive? Or too timid in your persuasiveness? Or have you found the correct balance?

4. Evaluate the response of your congregation to the preaching of the Word of God.

a. Is it usually presented authoritatively as the Word of God that is to be received and obeyed?

b. How would you describe the response of the congregation to the preached Word? Do they respond with obedience?

c. What factors and influences do you think cause the work of your pastor to be a joy to him? What causes him to feel at times as though it is a burden to him? Be sure that you discuss these matters openly and considerately together with him.

SECTION II

Fulfilling the Office of Elder

LESSON 1 – Leaders Who Equip God's People

Scripture Reference: Ephesians 4:1-16

All those who have ever served as Pastors or Elders in the local church are well acquainted with the stress that results from conflicting expectations that people have of us. We will never be able to satisfy everyone's expectations. We look instead to the expectations of the Lord of the Church as expressed in His Word. This is a strategic passage in which Paul, more than in any other, gives us his view of the task of spiritual leaders in the local church. They are to "… prepare God's people for works of service…." (v. 12) The word that Paul selects has an interesting medical history in classical Greek. It describes what a Greek physician would be doing when he puts a shoulder back into place, or corrects a broken leg, thereby putting it into a right relationship with the other parts of the body so that it fits thoroughly and can function as designed.

1. Reflect on vss. 3-6 very carefully and share your reflections with others on where you believe the real unity of the body of Christ is experienced.

2. Where do spiritual leaders get their right to lead? (Reflect on vss. 7-11, but remember that the offices mentioned in v. 11 are not permanent offices in the church).

3. Reflect carefully on v. 12 and discuss the following questions:

   a. Paul says that God's people must be prepared for "diakonia." What do you know about the word "diakonia" and what does it involve?

   b. What does this statement tell you about "God's people?"

   c. Someone has said that making such a sharp distinction between clergy and laity has taught most people to believe the average members of our churches are not very important. Would you agree?

   d. Do you see some of that happening in your church?

4. According to vss. 12-16 what are the marks of a church that is truly "built up?" See how many of them the group can list from this passage.

5. Evaluate the amount of time that you spend in your work as Elder. Then answer the following questions:

   a. How much of that time is "organizational time," that is, spent in meetings, with committees, and other such tasks?

   b. How much of that time is "pastoral time," that is, spent with people directly and in roles that are specifically designed to minister to people?

   c. In view of what v. 12 says about the task of a spiritual leader, are you satisfied that your time is being distributed well? or, does it need some rearrangement? If so, how?

6. Do you believe that your church looks like an "equipping church" that prepares God's people for works of service?

   a. Where do you think it is the strongest in this matter? Cite two examples.

   b. Where do you think we are the weakest? Cite two examples.

   c. What changes do you believe we should consider?

LESSON 2 – Leaders With Right Motives

Scripture Reference: I Peter 5:1-11

The terminology of "shepherd" and "flock" is familiar to most of us only because of our acquaintance with Scripture and its frequent usage there. But it is probably not very familiar to us in our experiences. We hardly ever see a shepherd, or a flock of sheep. But those who know tell us that sheep are very dependent creatures who cannot get along by themselves. While other animals can roam without supervision, sheep are certain to get into difficulty if left alone. They are particularly vulnerable to attacks by other animals and quite defenseless. They must, therefore, be taught to follow a leader and overcome their dangerous tendency to wander off in other directions.

1. God has called you to be an "undershepherd" of a portion of his flock. Do some more research and thinking about the nature of sheep, and take note of many of the parallels that you see in the local congregation. List them and then share your reflections with the others.

2. Peter speaks about the "glory" that shepherds will experience. Note verses 1, 4, 6, and 10. What is that? What glory do you expect to experience as an elder?

3. Peter makes it clear in vss. 2 and 3 that there are some elders in the church who carry out their office with impure motives.

   a. Is it easy for an elder to carry out his office only because he must and not because he is willing? Are you bothered by that temptation at times? When is it the strongest?

b. In what ways do you think ancient elders could use their office to satisfy their greed for money? In what ways is it possible to use the office for personal gain today, though it may be other gain than monetary? Can you think of any example of spiritual leaders today who have used their office for personal gain? What has happened to them and their ministry?

c. In what ways is it easy for elders to lord it over those who are under their care? How can we avoid that?

4. In verses 5-7, Peter speaks about the virtues of submissiveness and humility among spiritual leaders. Give an example from your experience of a leader who was exceptionally influential because of his humility.

5. Peter was writing these words to the scattered Christian churches who were going through tough times because of opposition raised against the cause of Christ. The devil was real to Peter, personally, and in the church.

a. Do you think the church you serve is conscious of the presence and intentions of Satan? Where do you see that?

b. What do you consider to be the two greatest temptations that spiritual leaders are confronted with today?

c. What are you doing to stand firm so that those temptations will not overcome you?

d. What do you consider to be the two greatest attacks
   that Satan is making against the Christian church today?

e. How well is your local congregation resisting those
   attacks?

f. In what ways should the total ministry of your church
   be improved so that you can be better equipped to
   resist Satan's attacks?

LESSON 3 – Leaders With Vision

Scripture Reference: Nehemiah 2:1-20

A University President once said that there are three kinds of people in the world—those who don't know what is happening, those who watch what is happening, and those who make things happen. Leaders, therefore, are the people who make things happen.

Not all leaders are in an office. But certainly those who are in an office of spiritual leadership ought to be people who make things happen. They must be people with vision, a mental picture of the way things should eventually be. Leaders who lead well live with a picture in their mind of how things should be next year and three years from now and even beyond that. Nehemiah was a leader who exhibited that qualification. As a civil leader who returned to Jerusalem to rebuild things after the Exile he showed himself to be a man with vision.

1. Nehemiah began with a realistic appraisal of present conditions. He had heard reports of what conditions were like back in Jerusalem, and he asked the king for permission to make an inspection tour.

   a. How much time do you spend as elders in realistic appraisal of the conditions of the church at present?

   b. What would you cite as the three most significant weaknesses of your local congregation at present? Can you reach a group consensus on that?

2. Nehemiah had a clear idea in his mind of exactly how he wanted the new city of Jerusalem to look.

   a. Spend a few minutes as a group sharing your ideas (dreams!) of what you would like your church to be like three to five years from now. This may well be the most important part of this entire lesson!

   b. Is there great diversity of ideas in your group, or were you pleased to find areas of consensus?

3. Nehemiah knew that carrying out a dream would require planning and organization. So he began to make notes about the materials he would need and how he would organize the people.

   a. What are the greatest resources and strengths your congregation possesses now for achieving your vision?

   b. How well is your congregation organized for ministry? Are the proper committees appointed? Do they function well? Are they accountable? Is some reorganization needed?

   c. Are the members of your congregation able to cooperate and work together toward significant goals?

4. **Many** visions seem impossible to achieve. That's when we're tempted to give up. Many of Nehemiah's companions may have felt that too. Cite three dimensions of your church's ministry that may have seemed impossible five or ten years ago.

5. It's one thing to have a vision. It's quite another thing to motivate others to work toward the accomplishment of that vision. How well does your council do at motivating the members of the congregation to work and build together? Where should that be improved?

6. All dreams will have enemies. Nehemiah found that out too.

   a. What are the obstacles that you will have to overcome as a church in order to achieve some of your dreams for the next five years?

   b. How will you begin doing that?

LESSON 4 – LEADERSHIP FOR PROGRESS

Scripture Reference: I Timothy 4:11-16

David Livingstone, the British missionary and explorer to southern Africa during the 19th century, once said, "I will go anywhere provided it's forward!" That spirit made him an outstanding leader. Leadership that goes nowhere, or backwards, is not true leadership. Paul frequently spoke of his own ministry as running a race and pressing on. Here he exhorts Timothy to the same and holds him up before us as a model. He is to apply himself in such a way that "... everyone may see your progress" (v. 15). Progress has two important dimensions to it. It's forward movement, but it's also supervised movement. To move forward, we must be able to look ahead. Leaders with a vision, therefore, are the only ones who can lead for progress.

1. Paul writes to the Philippians about their "progress and joy in the faith...." (1:25) and Peter exhorts his readers to "... grow in the grace and knowledge of our Lord and Savior Jesus Christ" (II Peter 3:18). Are you confident that you have experienced progress in your personal Christian life during the past couple of years? What kind do you observe?

2. What kind of progress do you observe in your church? Does the congregation desire progress, or are most of them very content to remain the same? If so, what can elders do to stimulate the desire for progress? What assistance can you give to your pastor so that his preaching will stimulate the desire for progress?

3. Paul has warned Timothy that there are many enemies of the church and that not all movement is progress. Consult I Timothy 4:1ff. and II Timothy 3:1ff.

   a. What are the threats that your church faces today?

   b. List what you consider to be the most important non-negotiables in the church, that is, matters on which there must be no change.

4. To exercise such leadership Timothy must be grounded in the Truth. Notice vss. 11, 13, and 16. Evaluate your own practice of the disciplines of the Christian life. How faithful are you in personal prayer and Bible study? How familiar are you with the Creeds and Confessions of the Church? Do you have a ready testimony for others?

5. Paul tells Timothy that his personal example is more important than his age (v. 12). (Timothy was probably about 35 years old at that time.)

   a. Evaluate the age spread among the elders in your church. Is age important to your congregation?

   b. What does it mean to set an example for others in our speech and life?

c. What does it mean to set an example for others in our love and faith?

d. Cite one example that you know of where leadership was damaged because of an impure life. What can we learn from that?

6. What gifts do you believe that God has given you for this task? What are you doing to develop those gifts now? Is there a possibility that you are neglecting them?

7. Leadership roles can be demanding. They require diligence and perseverance (cf. v. 15,16).

a. On what other activities have you cut back so that you can do justice to your work as elder?

b. What causes you the most frequent frustration and discouragement as an elder?

c. Do you often become "...weary in doing good...." (Galatians 6:9)? What do you do to overcome that?

LESSON 5 – Leaders With A Towel

Scripture Reference: John 13:1-17

To many today leadership is measured in terms of power. The two always seem to go together. However, every once in a while someone comes along who strikingly teaches us the opposite. A Mother Teresa forces us all to sit up and take notice that leadership is service, not power. Jesus did the same with the disciples in this passage. They never expected him to become the washer of feet. But he did! And then he called himself an example that they should follow. To do so must have caused them to rearrange their whole idea of what it meant to be a leader. Power is out! Service is in!

1. Do some research and study to discover their cultural practices concerning footwashing. How was footwashing usually done? Why was it done?

   a. Why do you think the disciples were surprised at what Jesus did?

   b. Why did Peter react the way that he did?

   c. How do you think you would have felt if you had been part of the group?

2. Jesus told them they should also wash each other's feet. (v. 14). You may never have accepted Foot-washing as another ceremony in the life of the church as some have. But what do you think Jesus meant when he said they should also do it to each other? List three lessons that you think he had in mind for us today.

   a.

   b.

   c.

3. Look around in your congregation, or perhaps in the district of the congregation for which you are responsible.

   a. Who do you see that would be in the category of needing their feet washed?

   b. Is it presently being done (whether in fact or in principle)? By whom? If it is not being done, who should be doing it?

4. Now look around you in the community in which God has placed your church.

   a. Who do you see in the community who needs this kind of a ministry?

b. How could it be initiated? What resources are available? Who could initiate it? What obstacles could be expected and how could they be overcome?

5. Describe two instances in which you took a towel (figuratively or in fact) during the past month to deliberately and lovingly minister to someone. Cite them for the group.

a.

b.

Remember that there are three ingredients in such a situation – the "dirt" that needs attention, the means that you use ("water"/"towel"), and a willingness to stoop low.

Note how all three have been present in your experiences.

the dirt –

the means –

the stooping –

6. Read what Jesus says in Matthew 20:26-28, and then explain what you think he meant, and what that means for us as elders today.

LESSON 6 – Worn-out Leaders

Scripture Reference: I Kings 19:1-18

This Old Testament story gives us very candid insight into the personal life of one of God's great prophets. He has just completed the victorious show-down on Mt. Carmel with the prophets of Baal. But suddenly everything collapses. He is depressed. He wants to die. This event has caused many to speak of the "Elijah Syndrome" that is a frequent trial of kingdom leaders. After great blessings and significant achievements, they become afflicted with a drabness of soul that destroys all motivation. Their work is discontinued, or done only perfunctorily. It seems only a visit from God will repair the situation.

1. Analyze the timing of this event in the life of Elijah. It happened right after the peak experience of chapter 18. Perhaps it is caused by fatigue. Or perhaps it is a direct counter-attack by Satan after a victory.

   a. Can you identify similar experiences in your life of service?

   b. Are you conscious of the fact that your pastor may be subject to those experiences periodically too?

   c. In what ways can you help one another as church leaders when such times of discouragement come?

2. God began to treat Elijah's needs by refusing to answer his prayer (v. 4). Can you cite instances in your life when God has blessed you by refusing to answer your prayers? Can you cite the same in the life of your congregation?

3. God sent an angel to Elijah. Do you think angels still function in the lives of Christians? What Biblical passages can you find that will speak about that? Are you conscious of times when angels have ministered to people in the church? and when they have ministered to you?

4. God was also concerned about Elijah's bodily care and gave him cakes and water (v. 5, 6). How well do you care for your physical health? Are you conscious that neglect of your physical health could affect your spiritual health, and then affect your ability to lead well?

5. God chose to speak to Elijah in a gentle whisper instead of a powerful wind, an earthquake, or fire. What do you think is the significance of that? When have you observed or experienced God speaking to you or others in a gentle whisper? Is it true that usually we look for the other more dramatic means of his speaking? Why?

6. It was necessary for God to correct Elijah's numbers. In his discouragement he had distorted the figures and drew the conclusion he was all alone (cf. v. 14 and 18). Can you think of times when we've made the same mistake in the church because of our fatigue and discouragement? How can we overcome the tendency to feel alone and forsaken in our roles of leadership?

7. Do you as elders have a ministry to one another? Are you conscious that some of your number are always battling the Elijah Syndrome? Are your relationships with each other loving and caring enough to be sensitive to that? Share with the others one time when a brother elder was particularly helpful in ministering to you.

Epilogue

I hope that these studies have helped you to sense that you have been placed in a very privileged position as an Elder in the Church of Jesus Christ.

The Church is very valuable to Christ. He prizes her above everything else and is working constantly to make her pure. Now, in His providence, and by the approbation of the other members of the congregation, you have been placed in a position of spiritual leadership in that body.

If you feel somewhat intimidated by that, use those feelings to cast you down before the Lord so that He may fill you will His strength. But don't ever shrink back from your work as an Elder. You are special! God has called you to a special role. Your fellow believers have expressed their trust in you. God has promised to provide the equipment for all the tasks He gives us.

You have just concluded a study of the nature and the function of that office. May God guide you to fulfill it humbly, faithfully, and courageously.

Paul's prayer for the Ephesians could be prayed for all the Elders of the church....

I pray that out of His glorious riches He may strengthen you with power through His Spirit in your inner being, so that Christ may dwell in your hearts through faith. And I pray that you, being rooted and established in love, may have power, together with all the saints, to grasp how wide and long and high and deep is the love of Christ, and to know this love that surpasses knowledge—that you may be filled to the measure of all the fullness of God.

Ephesians 3:16-19 (NIV)

Leader's Guide

This "Leader's Guide" is included here in order to provide assistance to those who will have the responsibility of leading the discussions on the office of Elder.

It ought to be repeated that these studies can take place in two very different settings.

* Some prefer to use these as a devotional session at the opening of each monthly Elders Meeting. My own use has followed this pattern. A half-hour is set aside at the opening of each meeting for this study. Whatever we cannot cover in that half-hour we carry over to the next month. In most cases that means one lesson for two months.

* Others prefer to study this matter in a workshop/retreat setting. When a day or more is set aside, away from formal agendas, the opportunity is there for much more indepth discussions and sharing. A number of lessons can be covered in one day and the result becomes cumulative.

In some settings the pastor will be the one responsible for leading these discussions. In other settings lay persons will be in charge and they will feel more comfortable in preparation if some additional guides are provided. Even where Pastors are present, it might be advisable and highly profitable if the responsibility of leadership is distributed among the group.

These guides are not intended to be comprehensive, but only to provide some additional insight, background information, or resources that will assist the leader.

The Nature of the Office

LESSON 1 – Appointed Elders

1. In your reflection on the circumstances among the people of Israel and Moses, remember that they were slaves at that time in Egypt. They were greatly increasing in numbers (Note Exodus 1:8-10 and the fact that by Exodus 12:37 they number 600,000 men besides women and children!). They were experiencing great difficulty (Note Exodus 1:11-22 and 5:1-21). God had called Moses to be their deliverer and because he was scared of the task, God put him through a special preparation process (Note Exodus 3:1-15).

   It is important to remember that Moses was not called to "appoint" the Elders of Israel. It's obvious they were already in existence as a group. He was to call on them for assistance. They were to help each other!

2. In looking for the charge that is given Elders when they are appointed, you will notice that no specific charge is cited in

Acts 14. It would be good for the group to reflect on what the church needed most from those Elders even though that's not spelled out.

In Titus 1 there are several references to the tasks of Elders. Note them in v. 9. The remainder of that section lists the personal qualifications of an Elder. You should note that many deductions can be made about their tasks from the qualifications that are necessary. Ask the group to do this.

3. In a comprehensive study on the nature of the office to which Elders (and Deacons) are called, the Christian Reformed Church addressed the matter of "laying on hands" in 1973. The Church was careful to say that the laying on of hands is not a sacrament, does not create a special priestly order of the church, and does not confer sacramental graces or mystical powers on the one ordained. However, it is a significant symbolic function by which the continuing officers publicly designate that these newly ordained persons have been set aside by God and the church for special tasks. If you desire more information concerning this study it can be found in "Report 44 – Ecclesiastical Office and Ordination," (pages 635-716), *Acts of Synod 1973,* Board of Publications of the Christian Reformed Church in North America. Other denominations have similar practices.

LESSON 2 – The Nurture We Provide

1. It will be necessary to engage the imaginations of the group on this one. It's so hard for us to identify with a shepherd because our experiences are so different. Urge them to exercise their imaginations so that they actually can see themselves as a Palestinian shepherd. Once they are in that frame of mind, then ask what they want to do for their sheep.

2. It would be wise to read Acts 19 in order to understand what Paul experienced in Ephesus. Paul established the church there during his three month stay. He spoke courageously in a wicked and pagan setting. He performed extraordinary miracles (19:11), aroused the opposition of many, and even endured a dangerous riot (19:23-41). During such circumstances, a leader exhibits what his character really is made of!

3. It is unimportant at this point which type of gospel presentation is used. Some prefer the "Four Spiritual Laws" published by Campus Crusade for Christ. Others prefer the presentation developed by Dr. D. James Kennedy (*Evangelism Explosion,* Tyndale). Many others are available from local mission boards. Others prefer to write their own based on their favorite gospel passages. What is most important is that Elders be familiar and comfortable with some always-ready presentation of the gospel, and that they are willing to reflect together on their experiences.

4. I would encourage you to use this as a group exercise. Each Elder should have notations in his personal Bible with such references so they are available at all times.

LESSON 3 – The Defensive Stance We Take

1. It is necessary for Elders to think very clearly about the threats that the church faces. There are some threats that are the same in all generations and your group ought to identify them clearly. Broken relationships, the tendency to cover up sin, self-centeredness, thirst for pleasure, lack of personal discipline, sexual immorality, etc., are timeless.

   However, we also ought to be able to identify those unique and particular threats that our generation faces which previous generations did not face. The drug culture, alcoholism, cults, abortion, homosexuality, child and spouse abuse, humanism, scientism, the fear of nuclear war, etc., are, to varying degrees, unique to our modern context. There are many more you could identify.

   It would be very healthy for your body of Elders to honestly admit to one another what circumstances in the church give them the greatest tears. Elders without tears will not be very well motivated in their work!

2. Be alert to the cleverness of Satan. Remember how that was exhibited already in Genesis 3. Try to identify some of these clever masquerades in our day.

3. This is a very critical question. Push the group to identify activities and stances among you that show you have a "wide-awake stance that will spot even the first appearance of danger and meet it." If you can't identify those ways, are you sure you are keeping watch?

4. In reflecting on this one, read and reflect on the danger Paul cites in Colossians 2:8. It is possible, he says, to be taken "captive through hollow and deceptive philosophy." We must be ready to clearly identify those dangers. You can't attack anything that you don't have clearly in focus!

LESSON 4 – The Corrective Care We Provide

1. As you study II Timothy 3:16, 17, it would be wise for the group to think about how frightening it is to be assigned a large task and not have the "equipment." Perhaps some of the group could express some feelings about that. Feelings of inadequacy are a gnawing fright to many.

   Here are the four forms of "usefulness" of the Scriptures:

   Teaching – the communication of God's revealed truth about himself, us, and the way of salvation.

   Rebuking – when we are sinful, rebellious, and in error, the Bible exposes that to us.

   Correcting – to lead us to a new course of thinking, feeling, believing and doing.

   Training in righteousness – to provide increased grounding with the ability to live productively, thereby staying on the new course established.

2. The purpose of this exercise is to allow Elders to draw on their own experiences, including both pain and profit, as a means of sensitizing them to what may be going on in their counselees. Since most folks don't accept admonition readily, patience is required. Yet because admonition continues to be necessary, Elders need the courage that comes from remembering that they come in the name of Christ.

3. This is a similar exercise designed to allow them to draw from previous experience, examine and evaluate it, and learn from it.

4. This can be an excellent group exercise to improve your personal skills in the practical use of the Word of God in your work as Elders.

5. Use this as an opportunity for the group to share with each other why the matter of confrontation is so difficult for many. Some fears are overcome by identifying them clearly. Others can be overcome through careful effort.

LESSON 5 – The Directional Leadership We Give

1. Notice that, after speaking about the unity of the body of Christ (vss. 1-6), Paul says that Christ has apportioned different gifts to different folks (vss. 7, 8). Notice also that vss. 9, 10 are a reference to the humiliation and suffering of Christ and his exaltation to Heaven that has given him the authority to distribute God's gifts to believers.

   Read vss. 11-13 very carefully, multiple times. Even have the group try to put it into their own words. This passage is critical for the understanding of the tasks of church leaders. Elton Trueblood referred to the pastor (and therefore Elders, too) as a "… 'playing coach,' sometimes carrying the ball himself and sometimes seeing to it that another carries it. Thus, he is both a minister and the encourager, a teacher and a developer of his fellow ministers, who are the members of the Church of Christ." (*The Incendiary Fellowship,* Harper & Row, p. 43, 44). You might want to discuss that viewpoint and what it says about how church leaders should lead.

2. The word Paul selects in I Timothy 5:17 has a picture built into it. The "director" is the person who stands before the crew of a ship at sea to coordinate their efforts as an able captain so that the ship may not only sail well but remain on course, or a conductor standing before a large orchestra coordinating the efforts of all the musicians so that harmonious music can be produced.

3. Walk through this passage verse by verse. Make a list of the qualifications. Be sure the group understands what they mean.

4. Take time for this one. Formulating a group definition of leadership could be a real growing experience. After putting some thoughts together you may want to reflect on it for a month, compare it with some other definitions, and return to its reflections next time.

5. Do these carefully. It may even be wise to spend a special evening, or an Elders' Retreat, on a planning session like this.

LESSON 6 – The Reception We Can Expect

1. You may find some Elders feeling somewhat awkward about being held in "respect and high regard." Remind them they do not receive such respect because of themselves, but because they come in the name of Christ as ordained persons. Consider what this infers.

2. You will have to bear in mind that the distinction between Elders and Pastors was often not a part of their experience in the New Testament Church. For the most part, that came later.

3. Group self-evaluation will require the freedom to be honest and open with one another. It will be healthy if your group can achieve that.

4. The intention here is not to open a discussion that will give all an opportunity to evaluate the pastor's preaching. Be sensitive to the fact that he may feel uncomfortable and even threatened at this point in the study. Repeat your commitment of support and shared responsibility to him. If there are sensitive matters concerning his preaching that some desire to express, they should be encouraged to do so privately first.

Do your best to make this an encouraging and supportive time for him. Spend some time giving him the opportunity to tell you about the joys, frustrations, and burdens his preaching ministry may involve for him. Ask him questions that will draw him out. You'll be able to help him more when you understand him better!

Fulfilling the Office of Elder

LESSON 1 – Leaders Who Equip God's People

1. Unity is, of course, desirable. How unified is your congregation? What criteria do you use to determine that? The group should agree on that first.

2. Remember that Ephesians 4:9 and 10 is a reflection of the humiliation and exaltation of Christ. The Ascended Christ now has the authority to send leaders to the church in his name.

   At the time Paul wrote to the Ephesians, they recognized apostles, prophets, evangelists, and pastor/teachers as the official leaders of the church. These are not permanent, and the list changes from time to time.

3. Ephesians 4:12 is a critical statement and needs to be understood carefully. Refer to the suggestion by Elton Trueblood that leaders are to be "playing coaches" (cf. the notes on Lesson 5 above).

4. After you've made the list, compare your evaluations of your congregation with this list.

5. Don't skip over this exercise too easily. It's important! The nature of most organizations is that we too easily spend more and more time organizationally and less and less time pastorally. But, that contradicts much of what the church is all about.

6. This exercise in evaluation of your congregation must be done honestly. Give enough time for it. It would be a good item for a Retreat setting too.

LESSON 2 – Leaders With Right Motives

1. This will require the use of some imagination again. Push them to do so. If someone has read Phillip Kellers, *A Shepherd Looks At Psalm 23* (Zondervan, 1970), it would be profitable to have him share with the group some insights gained about sheep and their behavior patterns.

2. Note that all Peter's references here to "glory" are in the future time frame. It's not glory now, but glory then! Do you suppose he's saying that those who desire their glory now will have only that? Think of the example of Christ Himself (cf. Philippians 2:5-11).

3. It would be helpful for the group to speak honestly about the temptations they face in order to pick up improper attitudes toward their task. They should also ask if there are some particularly modern temptations that elders in Peter's day didn't face.

4. If they're willing to share such examples it could be an excellent exercise in thanksgiving and encouragement.

5. This discussion will get your Elders right back to the basics. How real do they think Satan is? How conscious are they of his strategies? Then you can go the next step and do some thinking about the attitude of Satan toward church elders. If Satan is determined to destroy the church of Christ, and if Elders are committed to building and nurturing the church of Christ, that puts Satan and Elders on a collision course! Let your group identify how and where they observe and experience that happening. If they are unaware of it, some bigger questions have to be asked!

LESSON 3 – Leaders With Vision

1. It would be helpful to spend some time with the first few chapters of Nehemiah in your preparation for this lesson. Nehemiah apparently put a fair amount of effort into his appraisal work. In 1:1, 2 he says he interviewed people who could give him first hand information. In 2:11-16 we have the record of his inspection tours. We always need an honest appraisal of circumstances before we can understand where to begin. Too many Elders plunge into agendas without stepping back for "appraisal time."

2. This may be difficult for some because they are not accustomed to thinking ahead. But each member should be encouraged to verbalize his/her "dream" for this church.

3-6. Be aware that many good "dreams" never become "actual" because they fall into the big hole in between the two! This is the time to ask how effective we are in understanding and providing for the steps that are necessary to get us from "here" to "there."

LESSON 4 – Leadership For Progress

1. This question is of a very personal nature. Encourage each Elder to ask it of himself/herself. If some are willing and interested in sharing their responses with the group, it would be excellent.

2-3. Be careful that "progress" remains positive. To some, "progressive" may be suspect. Carefully avoid that, pointing out that growth, sanctification, and maturation are all progress. Those changes that violate our basic commitments are never to be considered progress.

4. This is an excellent time to remind all Elders that their own personal spiritual care must be their first priority. If they are not healthy spiritually, they cannot help others to become healthy. Perhaps a review of their ordination vows would be helpful at this point.

5. Age was a consideration in the early Christian Church. The word "elder" certainly reflects that. But the consideration of age seems less and less significant in many churches. It might be appropriate here to discuss what "eldership" signifies.

6-7. Personal priorities again enter the picture here. Elders should be encouraged to be firm in their commitments to office. Other activities will probably have to be cut back during the term of office. Encouragement will be needed from one another.

LESSON 5 – Leaders With a Towel

1. In their day feet were protected only by sandals and were at least partly exposed to sand and dirt. After walking on unpaved roads, feet were both dirty and very uncomfortable. In such circumstances, the washing of feet became a common and necessary practice. Providing the washing of feet was an act of courtesy and hospitality by a host. But because it was a menial task it was performed by a servant and never the host!

2. You should be sensitive to the fact that some traditions continue to practice foot-washing.

3-4. Again, engage in an analysis of the needs that are around you.

5. It's also good for us to look around and see the service that is provided. But, be careful! It's very easy to overlook the special acts of service. Don't miss them.

6. Read this passage carefully and notice that Jesus does not say it's wrong to desire "greatness." But he redefines what greatness is!

LESSON 6 – Worn-Out Leaders

1. It's very important to provide freedom for Elders, and for Pastors to admit that they have such times too. It will not help to think we must cover up such drab days so that we will appear "more spiritual" to our colleagues. Notice that "c" is the point at which we must arrive – with a commitment to help each other.

2. If you can tell of times when you have benefitted from unanswered prayers, then you will be able to minister well to others who wrestle with that disappointment.

3. The study of angels is a fascinating one. Look up Psalm 34:7, Psalm 91:11 and Hebrews 1:14 to cite just a few.

4-6. Take each of these ingredients in the process of Elijah's care and measure your own experience by them.

7. The assumption throughout much of this study is that Elders have the responsibility to minister to fellow Elders. Often we forget that. As colleagues we must carry a concern to pray for and encourage one another. Special times of prayer for one another should be included in your meetings.

www.ingramcontent.com/pod-product-compliance
Lightning Source LLC
La Vergne TN
LVHW051710080426
835511LV00017B/2826